Social Work 101

by
Symoné Miller, MSS, LCSW

Happy Reading!
Symoné C. Miller

ISBN: 978-1-7369480-0-2

Social Work 101

Proudly self-published through Divine Legacy Publishing, www.divinelegacypublishing.com

Dedication

This book is dedicated to my mother, Mary E. Kelly, the woman who has ALWAYS put my needs and wants ahead of her own. Mommy, you were one of the only people who supported me when I decided to pursue social work instead of nursing. You believed in me even when I questioned myself. I love and appreciate you more than I could ever express.

Acknowledgements

First and foremost, I have to thank God for giving me the passion to help His people. I am grateful to be able to use my gifts to help others who are interested in pursuing social work.

To my husband, Timon, thank you for supporting my writing journey and all my social work ventures. I appreciate you.

To my sorority sister, Arlene, thank you for always believing in me and holding me accountable each step of the way in writing this book.

Four years ago, I reached out to Amanda Chambers about writing a self-help book and life got in the way, but I have officially finished my social work self-help book which would have not been possible without you. Thank you for being my soror, writing coach, editor, and publisher.

To my fabulous illustrator, Mya, thank you for bringing my creative vision to life.

Speak up for those who cannot speak for themselves.

-Proverbs 31:8

Introduction

This year marks 10 years since I have been a social worker, and I can sum it all up with saying it has been a journey. Since the moment I stepped foot in the Introduction to Social Work course at Bloomsburg University to fulfill a general education requirement, I have continuously been drawn to the profession and everything it stands for. The journey of a social worker can rarely be put into words as there are an influx of emotions that I have felt over the years, from joy when clients are engaged and improving to frustration at systems that are not effective in helping my most vulnerable clients. All those emotions have made me the social worker I am today.

Looking back on my career, I would have loved to read a book that highlighted the social work profession and not just the success stories. I would have loved to read about how social workers gave their all and sometimes it still may not have been enough because at times that is the reality. Unfortunately, I did not have that experience when I was studying. It seemed like each book highlighted all the positive things that would happen with clients, not the realistic circumstances one may encounter whether it is a client refusing to meet with you, another denying there are any problems in their life at all, or even the client who is mandated to treatment to avoid legal consequences.

There are so many variations of what you can experience in the field and the myths about what we as social workers do on a daily basis. Working as a social worker requires ongoing critical thinking and quick assessment skills as things can change abruptly.

I wrote *Social Work 101* to share my perspective on the social work profession and for future social workers to gain insight into what they may experience. There may be days in which you feel unmotivated, frustrated, or inadequate because things are beyond your control but know we have all felt that way at one point or another. There will also be days when you sit in awe and embrace the small victories like a client saying thank you, securing housing for a client who has been homeless for years, or initiating a new program at an agency. It is important for you as future social workers to remember your why. Your why is the reason you entered this field. During the days in which you are experiencing a whirlwind of emotions, your why will keep you going.

It is imperative to take extremely good care of yourself mentally, physically, and emotionally. In this field you will have successes, but you will also see people at their lowest and most vulnerable points. It is also imperative to listen with an open heart and know that you do not necessarily have to agree with someone's decisions to do your absolute best to serve them as their social worker. This book shares the history of social work in America, the misconceptions of the field, things you wish you knew prior to becoming a social worker, and movies that allude to the social work profession. With Covid-19 cases steadily increasing on a daily basis, racial tension, and political unrest in the United States, the amount of individuals struggling with mental health is on the rise. This book was written out of necessity to highlight the importance of the helping professions, specifically social workers.

It is not enough to be compassionate. You must act.

\- Dalai Lama

Social Work

From the 1300s to the 1800s, England passed several Poor Laws due to having a large number of people who were unemployed which resulted in food scarcity. It was at that time that the Queen announced a new set of laws to keep order and contribute to the good of the kingdom. These laws were known as the Elizabethan Poor Laws and remained in place for more than 200 years. The Elizabethan Poor Laws created the government and laid out ways and a means to deal with dependents (beggars, the involuntary unemployed, and the helpless). The Elizabethan Poor Laws also separated people into two classes: the first one being the worthy which were those who were considered frail, elderly, orphans, handicapped, and widows. The other class was determined to be unworthy and were people who were considered lazy and alcoholics.

When settlers from England came to America, they brought their practices of aiding the poor which some would argue was developed to address the public's annoyance with begging instead of a true desire to address poverty. The Elizabethan Poor Laws had three categories of recipients: the able-bodied poor, the impotent poor, and dependent children. Several of the policies within the Elizabethan Poor Laws were embedded into the social welfare policies of America. It was the responsibility of the government to care for impoverished people, children who were orphaned, and those who were needy.

A young, college educated woman named Jane Addams, who had a commitment to helping those in need, found her passion while in London in 1888. While there she saw a settlement house that assisted poor workers by providing them with services. Addams was heavily impacted by what she witnessed and decided to bring this model to the United States during the early stages of migration. Just one year later, Addams founded the first United States settlement house in Chicago, Illinois named Hull House with an array of services like community activities, providing food and shelter to those in need, and offering referrals to outside agencies. Because of this, Addams is well known as the founder and pioneer of social work in the United States.

The primary professional organization for social workers is the National Association of Social Workers (NASW) which has defined social work practice as consisting of the "professional application of social work values, principles, and techniques to one or more of the following ends: helping people obtain tangible services;

counseling and psychotherapy with individuals, families, and groups; helping communities or groups provide or improve social and health services; and participating in legislative processes" with the following mission:

The primary mission of the social work profession is to enhance human well-being and help meet the basic human needs of all people, with particular attention to the needs and empowerment of people who are vulnerable, oppressed, and living in poverty. A historic and defining feature of social work is the profession's focus on individual well-being in a social context and the well-being of society. Fundamental to social work is attention to the environmental forces that create, contribute to, and address problems in living.

Social Workers are guided by their code of ethics and the core values of service, social justice, dignity and worth of a person, importance of human relationships, integrity, and competency. In terms of service, social workers are expected to serve those who are in need with their knowledge and expertise not only in a paid position but to also volunteer their expertise without financial compensation. Social workers are advocates and pursuers of change. It is important for social workers to advocate on behalf of those who are vulnerable, oppressed, and those who don't have the ability to do so while promoting social justice. Social workers are to always respect and honor the dignity and worth of a person, showing care and concern while being respectful of any diversity that may be present. Social workers understand and value human relationships, meaning they work collaboratively in a linear process through the helping process. The word integrity simply means moral uprightness and social workers are expected to act in this manner along with being honest and dependable. Lastly, social workers are to continuously seek additional opportunities to increase their professional skills and knowledge to build their level of competence.

There are three levels of social work: micro, mezzo, and macro. Micro means small therefore micro social work is primarily done on an individual level. This level of social work is the most common and consists of working with children in foster care, working with individuals to secure housing, and even providing individual therapy services. This level of social work is key in connecting clients to resources. Mezzo social work addresses the issues within a group system such as a family or community. On this level social workers create small scale cultural, institutional, and social change. Mezzo social work positions include working for an insurance company, a parenthood educator, or a community group leader. On the other end of the spectrum, macro social work explores problems on a larger scale. Macro social work focuses on not only developing but implementing interventions on a larger level while collaborating with other entities. Jobs in macro social work include community-based education initiatives, organizational leadership, policy analysis, and advocacy.

I am only one, but I am one. I cannot do everything, but I can do something. And I will not let what I cannot do interfere with what I can do.

- Edward Everett Hale

Social Work Education

If you are considering a career in social work, it is highly recommended that you review the Council on Social Work Education's website. The Council on Social Work Education is a national organization that represents social work education throughout the entire United States and ensures academic improvement, public accountability, and quality assurance within accredited social work programs. The Council on Social Work Education has a Commission of Accreditation which is a subgroup that develops the social work accreditation standards and ensures that schools are meeting these standards.

If you decide to attend and are able to successfully graduate from an accredited social work program, your degree will be recognized and respected within the profession making it easier to become gainfully employed. It is through this organization that you can explore social work programs that have accreditation according to their education level, whether they offer distance learning, and even their program contacts. As of October 2020, there are 533 accredited baccalaureate social work programs, 291 accredited masters of social work programs, 15 baccalaureate social work programs in candidacy, and 22 masters of social work programs in candidacy. There are also two baccalaureate programs in pre-candidacy and 17 master's programs in pre-candidacy. Candidacy is when baccalaureate and master's programs have applied for and are progressing toward full accreditation, but are not yet fully accredited by the Council on Social Work Education.

As with any potential career choice one would ask, what kind of job can I obtain with a Bachelor of Social Work degree? These job opportunities include case manager (behavioral health, substance use, intellectual disability, and truancy), crisis worker, assessment worker, service coordinator, foster care worker, intake worker, group home worker, residential counselor, program coordination, workshop director, and the list goes on. There are some states that offer BSW licensing, so check with your state licensing board to see if this is an option for you.

The Social Work National Honor Society, Phi Alpha Honor Society, was established in 1962 with six chartered chapters. There are now over 450 chapters with the organization continuing to grow. In order to become a member of Phi Alpha Honor Society, you must meet the academic requirements which are to rank in the top 35% of your class. Phi Alpha Honor Society offers the following: recognition of academic excellence, a membership certificate and lapel pin, national presentation opportunities, and a lifetime membership.

In order to complete a BSW program, you must complete an internship with a specific amount of hours of supervised field experience. An internship gives social work students an opportunity to gain on the job experience in a real-world setting. Whenever possible, it is recommended to secure an internship in your field of interest as oftentimes job opportunities can be offered to a student upon graduation. It is also encouraged to seek volunteer opportunities aside from your regular coursework as a future social worker to make yourself more marketable in the field and to build connections that can be lifelong.

While in undergraduate school, you may encounter graduate programs or your current school may even offer a Master's of Social Work degree. If you are interested in continuing to advance your career, it may be beneficial to make connections while pursuing your undergraduate degree with the idea that you may pursue a graduate degree. A major benefit of obtaining your BSW would be that you have the opportunity to obtain your MSW degree in less than one year if you meet specific requirements, such as specific grades in your social work courses, a cumulative grade point average, and/or an interview along with meeting the requirements for the two year MSW program (each MSW program requirements vary).

Since MSW students can have full time employment, there are a variety of program options including the previously mentioned advanced standing program that is designed to be completed in less than a year. This program allows students to forgo the first year of foundation courses that would have already been successfully completed in their BSW program. The full time program is designed to be completed in two years and the part time program is expected to be completed in three years with some programs offering a longer timeframe. MSW programs are continuously making attempts to accommodate the working professional with evening courses, weekend courses, and even offering all classes on one specific day to allow working professionals the opportunity to continue their employment. While enrolled in the MSW program, an internship is required along with a seminar course. This seminar course is designed to be a safe space to learn and grow from your peers, share your internship experiences, and focus on evidenced based practices and theoretical orientations.

Another benefit of obtaining a MSW is developing a specialization which can help you find your passion within the field. Specializations set you apart from your peers and can make you more marketable. Local crisis response centers primarily assess and refer clients to drug and alcohol and mental health services. Substance use is continuously evolving as a specialization with the opioid crisis across the country and the need for more qualified professionals to work with this population. It is important, if working with this population, to learn both inpatient and outpatient levels of care. This book will not highlight all levels of care but will emphasize the most common levels of care whose names may be different depending on the criteria being used in your state. Inpatient levels of care for substance use include detoxification and rehabilitation.

Detoxification level of care is utilized when a person is actively in withdrawal from a substance and requires 24 hour nursing care. Symptoms that are commonly used to meet criteria for this level of care include withdrawal symptoms from seizures, elevated vital signs, vomiting, and delirium tremors often known as DTs. These symptoms and a positive urine drug screen are indicators that the person could benefit from detoxification, which is an urgent level of care. An urgent level of care is one that is medically necessary and could be life threatening if not utilized. If a person meets medical necessity criteria for detoxification and decides that they do not need the treatment, they could potentially die from the substance withdrawal symptoms. Following the completion of detoxification, it is recommended that a person continue their recovery journey and transition to rehabilitation to have the best possible outcome of long-term sobriety. There are various types of substance use rehabilitation including short and long term, but both have the same goal of addressing a person's substance use and teaching relapse prevention skills. Depending on the severity of use and other factors, a longer stint in rehabilitation could be the most beneficial. Rehabilitation level of care is where individuals live at a facility, attend group and individual sessions, develop an understanding of their triggers for using, learn ways to cope with these triggers, and meet with a psychiatrist to address any mental health needs and to prescribe Medically Assisted Treatment. Medically Assisted Treatment is a combination of behavioral and counseling therapies and medication to treat substance use disorders. It is approved by the Food and Drug Administration and has been shown to successfully treat substance use disorder when combined with therapy.

Outpatient substance use programs vary depending on the state and county, but a common level of care is an Intensive Outpatient Program (IOP). An IOP program is designed to minimize the amount of time adults will have to miss work, school, or other obligations while still addressing their struggles with addiction. IOP programs offer individual and group therapy sessions, family sessions, incorporates mindfulness techniques, utilizes evidenced based practices, and can administer Medically Assisted Treatment (MAT). Something that I have noticed during my time working in the mental health system is that there appears to be a shortage of substance use services to adolescents although some people have admittedly started using substances in adolescence.

Mental health is another specialization with more than 200,000 clinically trained social workers, which is more than psychiatrists, psychologists, and psychiatric nurses combined. The Substance Abuse and Mental Health Services Administration (SAMHSA) states that social workers are the largest group of mental health service providers in the nation. When discussing the mental health specialization, we will discuss it from the most restrictive setting to the least restrictive setting. The most restrictive mental health level of care is inpatient hospitalization. There are two ways to be admitted to an inpatient psychiatric hospitalization: 1) voluntarily and 2) involuntarily. In order for a person to be admitted to a psychiatric hospitalization voluntarily, they would need to come to a facility (oftentimes a crisis response center or a hospital emergency room) presenting with symptoms that would either cause harm to themselves or other people. A person who is admitted voluntarily demonstrates an understanding and has insight into their need for treatment.

On the other hand, a person who is admitted to a psychiatric hospitalization involuntarily may have a different presentation. For instance, an involuntary admission may have attempted suicide and was found unconscious by a family member or may have said or did something that prompted their loved ones to pursue an involuntary petition. It is also possible for a person to voluntarily come to a crisis response center but later change their mind about being admitted to a psychiatric hospital. If the person is a danger to themselves and/or others, then the evaluating psychiatrist can file the petition for an involuntary commitment. While in inpatient hospitalization, a person will meet with the psychiatrist daily, receive individual and family sessions, group therapy sessions including creative arts, and have nursing staff and mental health technicians 24 hours a day to ensure their safety. Prior to discharge from acute inpatient, an aftercare plan is set up to include a follow up appointment with a psychiatrist, sometimes a therapist, or an acute partial hospitalization program.

Acute partial hospitalization is another level of care that can be utilized once a person leaves acute inpatient hospitalization. When attending an acute partial hospitalization program, a person goes to the facility daily from approximately 9am to 5pm. While there they receive group and individual therapy and meet with a psychiatrist for ongoing medication management. This level of care can be utilized for someone who needs further stabilization upon discharging from inpatient hospitalization but no longer meets medical necessity for an inpatient hospitalization. Another aftercare plan may consist of what is commonly called traditional outpatient treatment. This level of care includes an intake appointment at either a mental health facility or a private practice. It can be followed by a psychiatric appointment which one can decline if they choose. Although medication is not required, it may be presented to continue to treat symptoms related to the reason for the hospital admission.

Children and adolescents present to hospitals and crisis response centers with various stressors related to school, their home environment, abuse, and neglect. If the youth is under a specific age (varies depending on the state) a parent or legal guardian must consent to treatment prior to the youth being admitted to a facility. If the youth is currently in any type of placement, then the legal guardian must be found prior to admitting the youth. This can be a barrier if the support person who brought the youth does not know who the legal guardian is at the time. For instance, if a youth is at school, attempts suicide, and is then rushed to the hospital with their school counselor for medical clearance, then is evaluated by a psychiatrist and determined to need inpatient hospitalization, the legal guardian would need to be contacted. The school counselor may not know that the child is currently living with their grandparents because of their mother's inability to care for them. If the grandparents do not have legal guardianship, it can become extremely complicated to place a child who is not old enough to consent to treatment without their guardian and poses legal consequences. Unfortunately, this barrier may leave children waiting while the hospital social worker tries to find a resolution.

Gerontology is another social work specialty. Geriatric social workers work with older adults to coordinate services in various settings. Geriatric social workers can work at the county's Area Agency of Aging conducting assessments to determine the number of services that would be the most appropriate for the older adult. Once that is completed, a geriatric social worker could work as a service coordinator to ensure that all the home-based needs are being met from home care, mobile delivery of meals, and even day programs to ensure not only their basic needs are met but that their psychosocial needs are being addressed. According to the National Council on Aging, roughly 1 in 10 Americans aged 60 or older have experienced some form of abuse including physical abuse, sexual abuse, emotional abuse, confinement, passive neglect, willful deprivation, and financial exploitation. In the event that this occurs, an ombudsman can investigate. An ombudsman role is to investigate and attempt to resolve complaints. Geriatric social workers are also employed at nursing homes and assisted living facilities to coordinate admission and discharge planning, develop programs for social interactions, and for therapeutic support.

Child welfare is one of the most well-known areas of social work possibly because these are the cases that tend to be publicized. Child welfare simply means ensuring that the needs of children are met, often focusing on cases where there is suspected abuse and neglect. Potential employers include the Department of Human Services, children and youth agencies, permanency and foster care, and family-based services. Child welfare social workers can also work within foster care agencies and residential placements to address the residential, behavioral, and social needs of children and adolescents. Social workers can work in areas of early childhood intervention and play a pivotal role in connecting children and parents to the most appropriate resources.

Medical social workers work in various medical settings including hospitals, health clinics, dialysis centers, and specialized medical facilities. Medical social workers who specialize in areas such as dialysis or cancer educate both clients and their families about the diagnosed medical condition, facilitate groups and individual sessions, complete paperwork for benefits, coordinate transportation, and other services. These social workers are responsible for managing the emotional, spiritual, mental, and financial effects of these medical conditions. Social workers who work in emergency rooms settings can be faced with a variety of scenarios from physical trauma such as gunshot wounds to sexual abuse to a suicide attempt. These social workers must be well-versed in multiple areas of the field as there is no predictor as to what they will experience. Healthcare social workers can work in community health clinics providing support and services to individuals, families, and the community. A part of their job responsibility would be connecting clients to resources and assisting them in completing paperwork for insurance or services such as medications. These social workers promote health, offer support groups, and educational services about public health.

Aside from the specializations listed above, social workers can also work as consultants. As a consultant, social workers can be employed as a program evaluator. In this role social workers are expected to review programs for satisfactory measures, innovation, operational research, and program planning. It is also expected that social work consultants evaluate programs to identify both strengths and weaknesses and develop a plan to build on the strengths and further develop those areas of improvement. Since the entire social work profession is focused on highlighting the client's strengths, it is only befitting for a social worker to work as a motivational/empowerment speaker. This role allows for a limitless amount of creative expression with the focus on a broad range of topics from self-awareness, women's empowerment, developing leaders, ethics, career advancement, entrepreneurship, teamwork, generational poverty, and oppression.

Who is more appropriate to teach a social work course than a social worker with direct field experience? The answer is simple, NO ONE. Contrary to popular belief, social workers can become professors at the collegiate level with a master's degree although some may argue that a doctorate degree would provide more opportunities. Social workers can teach introductory courses in social work, specialty courses, and even become field liaisons supporting social workers to be in their field placement. Learning from experienced social workers in the classroom has undeniable benefits which include learning from someone with direct experience, developing a relationship with faculty, networking opportunities, improving research skills, and obtaining letters of reference.

Social workers who are interested in research work on the macro level with four primary categories: quantitative and qualitative research and primary and secondary research. Qualitative research is collected by open-ended questions and conversations. On the other hand, quantitative research is collected by more standard measures like surveys and questionnaires. Primary research is data collection collected first hand by the researcher while secondary research is data collection gathered by organizations. No one category of collecting research is considered better than the other, but one may be more useful depending on the topic and the amount of people you are collecting information from. Not only are researchers interested in collecting data but they utilize this data with a hypothesis already created and the data will be tested to see if the hypothesis can be proven. This research should be used to build the knowledge base of the social work profession and solve both practical or social problems.

Hospice social workers specialize in end-of-life care. These social workers are highly trained in bereavement and working with health systems. Hospice social workers work collaboratively with a team to help the team understand the emotional and psychosocial factors related to the client's care. Two of the goals of hospice social workers are to decrease the burden on families and provide support. Hospice social workers often meet with clients and their families to make end of life decisions based on the client's desires. It is the responsibility of the social worker to advocate for the client's wishes while empowering them to share their fears. They also identify community resources to help both the client and their family. As in many other social work roles, hospice social workers help clients complete necessary paperwork for insurance and even assist with funeral planning. Hospice social workers mediate conflict, provide counseling with the identified client and their families, and educate the community as the need arrives. Contrary to popular belief, hospice does not necessarily mean sadness for some clients and their loved ones as they can view this time as allowing their loved one to be free from pain and be at peace.

School social workers facilitate workshops and obtain and coordinate resources to meet the needs of students. School social workers are responsible for collaborating with school administrators and teachers to explore the root of a child's distress. Working in this capacity will allow a social worker to counsel students individually, in a group, or in a family setting to address the personal and psychological issues that may be affecting them. Social workers participate in individualized educational planning meetings, provide crisis intervention services, assist with conflict resolution and anger management, identify and report suspected child abuse and/or neglect, and work collaboratively with parents to locate resources for children with special needs.

Perinatal social workers work with an individual or family before conception begins until the infant's first birthday. These perinatal social workers can help with some of the following issues: drug use with the pregnant woman or her family, medically high-risk pregnancies, family conflict, legal concerns, poverty, grief and loss (infertility, miscarriage, stillbirth, and death), and with parents who have cognitive, behavioral, or mental health needs. Perinatal social workers are in place to support the woman with navigating the health system, advocating for not only the woman but the infant's well-being, and accessing financial assistance and support within the community. Social workers can also work in maternal wellness as a midwife, a doula, or a lactation specialist. A midwife is a person who is trained to assist a woman delivering a baby at a hospital, birthing center, or at home. A doula is seen as a birth assistant or a person who offers emotional, mental, and physical support to the mother. A lactation specialist is a person who specializes in breastfeeding and breastmilk. These careers in maternal wellness may require additional training or certifications for advanced competency.

Since social workers have been formally trained to work with systems, advocate for the oppressed, and have written communication skills, a social worker could work as a grant writer for social service agencies, advocacy organizations, or even legislation. Since many non-profit agencies rely on grants for specialized funding to expand their programs, a grant writer is expected to research grant opportunities that align with the mission and values of the agency. After the initial research is completed, the grant writer will write the proposal, which may include community endorsements and the developed plan for how the money would be spent along with its potential benefits. If the proposal is approved for grant funding, the grant writer may be asked to provide a summary of the benefits of the grant.

According to the United States Veterans Affairs website, Veterans Affairs (VA) is the largest employer of social workers and has been integrated in all programs offered by the VA. The role of a social worker for the VA is to not only treat mental and medical issues but is actively working to address all areas of the veterans life. Social workers provide counseling for veterans and their families, case management services, crisis intervention, assessment, and treatment of substance use services and linkages to additional support.

Advocacy is at the core of the social work profession, so there is no surprise that social workers can be employed as advocates. Their role includes advocating for what is in the best interest of their client. For instance, a victim advocate may screen and access for potential domestic violence, coordinate care management services, or provide services for the victim and their families along with providing community education. A child advocate focuses on the well-being of the child and can educate the community about ways to prevent child abuse. Child advocates conduct home visits, attend court hearings, collaborate with other stakeholders, support trauma survivors in court, and connect children who have been impacted by trauma to specialized resources such as therapy and support groups.

Each state varies in the qualifications needed to independently practice therapy and the highest licensure level for social workers is the Licensed Clinical Social Worker (LCSW). In order to become a LCSW, a person must first obtain their master's degree in social work and then must practice clinical work with supervision (hours and frequency may vary depending on the state in which you reside, consult your local social work board for clarity). Also, as a LCSW, you can become credentialed with insurance companies to bill directly for therapy sessions. Upon initially meeting with a LCSW, an intake evaluation is completed where the LCSW will ask a series of questions to get to know you better while assessing you and then work on collaborating with you for a parallel process to develop treatment goals using evidenced-based practices. An LCSW can diagnose emotional, behavioral, and psychological disorders. LCSWs are also excellent candidates for employment at managed care insurance companies due to their wealth of clinical knowledge and in utilization review for agencies. Utilization reviewers are an integral part of the treatment team in bed-based levels of care because they are responsible for relaying to the insurance company the need for continued treatment and explaining how medical necessities are being met.

Social workers bring a unique set of skills to any career as they have a great deal of experience in both written and oral communities, can express empathy, are knowledgeable about community resources, and have experience advocating for underrepresented communities. With the previously stated skills, social workers thrive in leadership roles from being the director of an inpatient psychiatric unit, to a supervisor in a behavioral health agency, to even being an executive director of an organization.

The happiest people I know are those who lose themselves in the service of others.

- Gordon B. Hinckley

Misconceptions About Social Work

One of the most common misconceptions about social workers is that they primarily work in child welfare and take kids away from their parents. As previously stated, social workers work in a variety of settings making child welfare one of many. Although social workers help facilitate the move of children from their parents when necessary, it is not their objective. It is actually more work for social workers to remove children but instead the goal would be keeping children in their homes while providing resources to improve their quality of life. Social workers do not have the authority to remove children based on their expertise but instead must receive permission from a judge who would grant this in extreme circumstances of neglect and/or abuse.

Once children are removed from their homes, the social worker has to make sure they are placed in a viable home, sometimes with family which is called kinship care, whenever possible. Sometimes, if there is more than one child, they could be separated due to the temporary placement limitations to take all the children. This can be traumatic for children not only being separated from their parents and their home but to also be separated from their siblings. Child welfare social workers work alongside the parents, the children, and the new caregivers to ensure all needs are met with the ultimate goal of reunification. Social workers may also work with the school system to ensure that the child(ren)'s educational needs are being met along with connecting the parents and their children to psychological support. In the event that reunification is not a viable option, the social worker will work to find a permanent placement for the children with no guarantee they will be placed together.

Social workers in the field have had the experience of initially shying away from social work because of the misconception that social workers do not make any money. It's easy to say, "It's not what you make, it's what you do with it," but the reality is that money makes the world go around, meaning it is needed to have a relatively decent life. If you are passionate about something, study your craft and the money will follow. With that being said, there is plenty of money to be made as a social worker in a variety of fields. There are social workers with bachelor's degrees in entry-level positions that make $35,000 and there are social workers who make over

$100,000 depending on their location, licensure, specialization, and amount of time in the field.

Society portrays this image that social workers are people who just want to help therefore anyone can be a social worker which is not true. You can help people in multiple professions, but there is much more depth to being a social worker than just helping. According to Merriam Webster, social work is defined as any of various professional activities or methods concretely concerned with providing social services and especially with the investigation, treatment, and material aid of the economically, physically, mentally, or socially disadvantaged, but let's go a step further with saying that social work is about transforming a system and empowering oppressed, underrepresented, and vulnerable people. Although social work's initial intent is to provide resources for vulnerable populations, it has expanded beyond economic circumstances. It is a broad field that is rooted in education, advocacy, and social justice.

Society also perceives that social workers are women only. According to Data USA, there are nearly 871,000 total social workers in the workforce with an average age of 42.3 and the average salary of $46,285 in 2017. There is a gender gap with over 80% of employed social workers being female according to the Bureau of Labor Statistics in 2015. Articles have been published that propose that the reason why there are fewer males in social work is related to lower status and salary in comparison to other professions. The average salary for a male social worker is $47,721 and $45,953 for the average female salary. Social work has grown 2.32% from 850,907 people in 2016 to 870,626 people. Males make up nearly 164,000 compared to 707,000 female social workers. Based on the data collected, 58.4% of social workers are white (Non-Hispanic) and 20.6% of social workers are Black (Non-Hispanic). It is unknown if this data is taken from people who directly work in the social work field or those who also have a degree in social work. Social work employment is expected to grow 12 percent from 2014-2024 according to the United States Bureau of Labor Statistics, therefore males in social work will have even more opportunities in the upcoming years.

Another misconception is that social workers only work with people of color since this is the population that needs help. This is completely wrong. Social workers work with all systems from individuals, families, and community from conception to death. It helps to have a social worker that looks like you. For instance, if you are working with a black adolescent who is having difficulties at home and at school, it may be challenging for this child to feel comfortable opening up to a white woman who is old enough to be the child's grandmother. The child may perceive the older white social worker as having nothing in common with them. Instead, it may be a sign of relief when the adolescent sees a black woman in her 20's standing at her door asking to meet. Not only is there a cultural barrier but historically social workers were not necessarily available to help but were seen as a system that would punish and reprimand instead of assist.

In terms of therapy and counseling services, there is a stigma in the black community that white people go to therapy and black people go to church which has resulted in the black community neglecting their mental health needs. This misconception has led to suffering in silence among people who have generations of trauma and oppression. Historically, in the black community, church was seen as a community that believes heavily in Jesus Christ and that therapy was not needed. Contrary to popular belief, it does not have to be either religious beliefs or therapy services. The two can co-exist and flourish when combined. There are social workers in agency settings and private practice who practice from a religious or spiritual framework and specialize in implementing both spiritual beliefs and therapy interventions to maximize the benefits of treatment. Culturally, the benefits and investment of therapy is not broadcasted and is significant.

There is a perception that once social workers have earned a clinical license they can only practice therapy, but there are other employment opportunities that require clinical social workers. Once a clinical license is earned, social workers will become more marketable and can become credentialed with insurance companies which can allow for billing at a higher rate. With that being said, clinical social workers may offer a sliding scale to clients. A sliding scale is a reduced rate offered to clients at the social worker's discretion. A sliding scale is used to help make quality therapy services accessible to everyone including those with financial limitations. For instance, an unemployed woman with a history of trauma may have difficulty finding a qualified therapist that accepts her insurance and has open availability. A clinical social worker may offer a sliding scale to this woman due to her unemployment status and limited social support. There are instances where a sliding scale may be less than a person's insurance copay depending on the type of plan they have. Clinical social workers have even offered pro bono sessions on a case by case basis.

As in other professions, social work can pose a work life and personal life balance conflict. Social workers can be torn between their desire to be there for their clients and the demands of their families. Social workers are known to have a demanding career serving clients often times outside of traditional business hours but also have families of their own. The reality is that social workers have to be mindful not to put all their efforts and energy into their professional careers that they neglect their own families if they have or want them. Ways to create a work/personal life balance include leaving the office at a reasonable time, not answering your phone after hours unless you are on call, being present with your loved ones, and learning to set healthy boundaries with clients.

As we lose ourselves

in the service of

others, we discover

our own lives and our

own happiness.

-Dieter F. Uchtdorf

What You Wish You Knew

Burnout is real! It is a level of exhaustion that can be coupled with hopelessness, compassion fatigue, loss of motivation, poor boundaries, lack of self-care, difficulty with sleeping patterns, poor concentration, irritability, health problems, the use of unhealthy coping skills, symptoms of depression, and anxiety. There are two simple words that can help prevent burnout among social workers and they are self-care. The term self-care is seen as some complex goal that is difficult to obtain, but in reality self-care is essentially creating and maintaining healthy boundaries and doing things that make you feel like yourself. One of these boundaries could be as simple as taking a regular lunch break. Social workers spend their days caring for the needs of others, and they may eat their lunch while on hold with the social security office for their client awaiting benefits if they have time to eat their lunch at all. No one should question your commitment as a social worker by your desire to step away from your desk and eat lunch without simultaneously working.

Another boundary could be using your sick and vacation time. So many times social workers push through their sickness by coming to work for their clients. They may also be concerned that there will be more work when they return or even that there will be consequences if they are out, but it is important for social workers to utilize their earned time to take care of themselves. When social workers are sick, it is necessary for them to visit their medical professional, get some much needed rest in bed, or take a "mental health day" to recuperate from their daily stress. The reality is that if something happens to you and you are unable to work, your job will have your position posted in the blink of an eye because it's a business, so as a social worker you have to handle your business and take care of yourself by practicing self-care. Self-care is also building a life that does not require escaping. By being intentional you are creating healthy habits and a lifestyle that should require minimal self-care.

Social workers can carry a steadily increasing caseload in regards to the numerical number, but it must be taken into account that these caseloads can require an extensive amount of footwork. This can also lead social workers to experience their own emotional effects of working with these clients during some of their most challenging times, which is known as vicarious trauma. Vicarious trauma can impact the performance of a social worker as well as their emotional stability. With all those dynamics, it is extremely helpful that social workers are offered and seek supervision which should be routinely offered from their employment agency. If a social worker is not directly employed by an agency, a peer consultation group could be beneficial to review cases, explore feelings of countertransference, and even just receive overall support.

Supervision is also required for social workers who are seeking clinical licensure. The question remains: "What do we talk about during supervision?" Of course, this time will be used for case reviews, but this time should be utilized for much more. Ethical issues including boundaries, diagnostic skills, interventions, cultural competence, work-related stressors, career goals, and self-care should be discussed. A supervisor's role is to not only focus on your caseloads, but it is their responsibility to look out for potential ethical violations, learning opportunities, encourage self-care and boundary setting, and to help social workers develop their career trajectory.

Another recommendation by social workers who have been in the field for years would be incorporating the Six Dimensions of Wellness, which according to the National Wellness Institute are: emotional, occupational, physical, social, intellectual, and spiritual wellness. Emotional wellness focuses on self-awareness of feelings, the ability to manage these feelings, and the ability to cope with stress. Occupational wellness focuses on personal enrichment and satisfaction through work which is simply defined as one's attitude about work. Physical wellness focuses on the importance of using food as medicine. The foods and substances that are put in the body ultimately influence how the body functions. Enhancing your physical wellness with physical activity whether it be cardio exercise, walking, or lifting weights can lead to overall wellness. A healthy balance of food with minimal processing, along with physical activity, will fuel your body to perform to its maximum capacity.

Social wellness focuses on how you interact with other people. To have optimal social wellness would mean that your social needs and desires are being met.

Social wellness highlights how one contributes to their community and overall harmony within the community. Intellectual wellness focuses on intellectual stimulation. This can be done with formal education through schooling or a training program or informal education, such as taking an interest in a hobby through reading books, magazines, or video tutorials. Lastly, spiritual wellness focuses on finding purpose in your life. Religious or spiritual beliefs can be included, but they are not required to have spiritual wellness.

The term "healthy boundaries" has been used throughout social work programs but can often be difficult to implement for a social worker. Jobs often act as if they expect social workers to put their client's needs above their own, which is understandable but this does not mean that social workers cannot implement strong boundaries such as leaving work on time whether it be leaving the office or a client's home on time. Of course, it would be rude to just run out of a client's home as soon as the clock strikes five o'clock, instead when entering the home at four o'clock they can begin their visit with the family by stating that the session should be 45 minutes. In doing this, it is creating an expectation of when you will be leaving so the client can be prepared for the allotted time. It is the responsibility of the social worker to remember the reason for their visit, redirect the conversation if necessary, and be mindful of their time constraints. This will take some time to master but it is imperative to create a healthy work life balance by leaving your work at work on time.

Another healthy boundary is simply taking your lunch break and whatever other breaks you are entitled to at your job. Employers have built your salary around you taking these breaks so be sure to do so. Taking breaks at work can help you retain and process information and be more productive. Healthy boundaries include physical, sexual, and emotional aspects as well. Although interactions with clients are often intimate and intense in nature, it is important for social workers to maintain physical boundaries that are comfortable for them, respectful of their clients, and to verbalize when these physical boundaries are being compromised.

Ethics are discussed in various social work courses, but one ethical violation that is a clear breach is having a relationship with your current or former clients. Some professions put a time limit on when the professional may be able to have a relationship with the client, but social work does not recognize that. If as a social worker you have a client, you cannot ever be in a relationship with them. It may be said that this is unreasonable, but as a social worker we are often seeing clients at some of their most vulnerable points in their life and we are not allowed to capitalize on that and become romantically involved.

Emotional boundaries have been more of a challenge for social workers who have worked on a long term basis with clients which may prompt the social worker to become more relaxed with their boundaries. It is necessary for social workers to refrain from blurring the lines and creating any kind of dual relationship because it jeopardizes the therapeutic relationship and can ultimately hurt the client. For example, if you are meeting with a client and they ask you a personal question, it may be appropriate for you to answer the question or to ask about the root of the question. Sometimes clients want to know about their social worker, which is understandable, but social workers should share only what is necessary to benefit the client. For instance, if you are meeting with an older client who asks you your age stating, "How would you be able to help me when you are as old as my grandchild?" Instead of stating your age, it may be more appropriate to share your previous work history, certifications, and overall willingness to learn about the client's concerns with older adults. It is always the responsibility of the social worker to not only set but also maintain boundaries.

No matter how organized you may consider yourself to be, it may be helpful to have a paperback planner to write down all your client's appointments and your own deadlines. In today's age of technology some have opted to move towards a virtual calendar, but whatever you choose stick to it as it gives you accountability. Organization is also an essential skill to maintain as a social worker to prevent any clients "falling through the cracks." This simply means reducing the risk of overlooking a client's needs and being the best possible social worker for each of your clients. Maintaining organization can prevent oversight and neglecting your clients, which can have detrimental consequences.

How many times have you heard the saying, "If it's not written down, it didn't happen?" This saying is a common theme in social work, but it has its accuracy. Documentation is a fundamental practice working in the field, and it is necessary. In the event you are unable to maintain a caseload for personal or professional reasons, someone else should be able to pick up your caseload and know exactly what is going on. An example of this would be a social worker working on a case for six months with a family composed of a single mother and three children under the age of 5 who live in a domestic violence shelter after being exposed to domestic violence at the hands of the youngest child's father. The case has legal involvement due to suspected physical and sexual abuse. If a social worker has neglected to write contact notes for the past three months and is involved in a car accident over the weekend where they cannot return to work for at least six weeks and the social work supervisor has to temporarily reassign these cases, the new social worker would be clueless as to what is going on with this family. Not only does this put the newly assigned social worker at a disadvantage by not having a "warm handoff" of the caseload, meaning being briefed by the former social worker about what is going on with the case, but now the newly assigned social worker cannot reference the documentation to be abreast about what is going on with this family. The lack of documentation written down not only impacts the social workers at the agency but more importantly this impacts the family who may be asked repetitive questions about their past and have to relive painful memories prompting possible distrust and questioning of incompetence on the newly assigned social worker's behalf. Working with the mindset that your documentation can be audited at any time will teach any social worker not to get ready but to always be ready.

The term work life balance is described as one finding a balance between the demands of work and the time allocated for other components of their life. This term does not necessarily mean that work and your personal life are equal but rather balanced. These other areas of one's life could be family, social, recreational, and/or educational. Having a work life balance makes you more productive, creates a reduction in stress, improves personal growth, increases happiness, and improves your overall wellbeing. By doing this, a social worker's risk of burnout can significantly decrease, which can lead to social workers remaining at an agency longer.

If you are looking for a career with concrete structure then you may want to rethink social work because it requires you to be flexible. A social worker may go to work on Monday expecting to follow up on a few cases and find out that a youth client had an emergency over the weekend requiring them to be removed from the home. It is at that moment that this youth's case takes priority because it would be considered an emergency. Social workers must be able to easily shift their focus and work with clients who are in emergency situations first to ensure their safety.

Licensure varies depending on your level of education and from state to state. There are different regulations in each state for clinical social workers to practice psychotherapy independently. For the most accurate and

Symoné Miller

up to date information about licensure, contact your state licensing board or visit their website. After obtaining a social work license you are required to obtain continuing education units (CEUs). CEUs are state board approved educational trainings that are given depending on the hours of the training. These trainings cover a variety of topics from ethics, substance use, different psychotherapy techniques, and much more. Some states also require specific CEUs such as ethics, suicide prevention, and child abuse to be completed within the renewal period. Social work licenses are renewed every two years (depending on your state) and all required CEUs must be obtained within that time frame. The social work state board may not ask for verification of CEUs at the time of renewal, but they conduct random audits so it is necessary for social workers to not only keep a copy of their CEU certificate but also a description of the training for their records. If you are ever audited, copies of these papers would be used to verify that you met licensing renewal guidelines.

Compassion fatigue is a fairly new term that is also referred to as vicarious trauma or secondary trauma. Social workers can experience emotional distress from working with clients who have experienced trauma. When working with these clients, social workers listen to their stories attentively and empathetically but with that listening social workers can experience compassion fatigue. Symptoms of compassion fatigue include anxiety, feeling overwhelmed, apathy, disorientation, isolation, hopelessness, poor self-care, sadness and grief, nightmares, and somatic complaints. A major thing every social worker should know is that you can't solve everything. Although many social workers get into the field to be change agents and to make a difference, it is equally important to know that you have limitations and recognize that making an impact on one client or one family is being a change agent.

Within the field of social work there are countless cultural implications, especially when social workers are in more reactive roles instead of proactive roles. In the African American community, social workers are not necessarily viewed as helpers, but they are viewed as people who are coming to take children away instead of people who are available to provide resources and help individuals, families, and communities improve their quality of life. Social workers are often the ones sent in when there is neglect and/or abuse within the home. When the guardian hears a social worker on the phone or sees the social worker at their door, their guard can immediately go up as they fear the social worker breaking up their family. This is a major barrier in helping a family when the family is guarded, therefore the social worker is unable to build rapport and offer valuable resources. It is also necessary for social workers to be adequately trained to engage with clients, especially those who are not particularly interested in engaging with them.

It is not your job to save everyone. Some people are not even ready to be helped. Focus on being of service to those who are, and be wise and humble enough to know when the best service you can offer is to guide them toward help in another direction.

-Anna Taylor

Boundaries

During social work coursework, boundaries are mentioned but this section of the book will highlight specific violations of boundaries and how social workers can navigate these situations to prevent a potential boundary violation. For example, social worker in her mid 30s is working in case management and has a female client in the same age range. During interactions, the client mentions social media to the social worker and even shares her desire to have additional friends. Weeks later, the social worker notices a friend request from the client. Initially the social worker thinks that it is not appropriate to befriend her client due to obvious reasons, such as the potential for dual relationships from case manager and client to friends due to the nature of information shared on social media including pictures of family, friends, and vacations. The social worker also thinks that declining the request may be detrimental to the therapeutic relationship as the client has a history of feeling abandoned by those she trusts.

Although the social worker does not have ill intentions, it is the social worker's obligation to maintain boundaries which should be clearly identified in the beginning of the relationship. This can be done during the initial meeting where the social worker discusses agency protocols. In an incident like this, the social worker can be proactive and mention this in supervision to have documented evidence of potential boundary issues, but the social worker also needs to be direct and share with the client the importance of maintaining boundaries, which includes that accepting a friend request on social media that will create a dual relationship and can negatively impact their therapeutic relationship. The social worker should be assertive in her approach but should also reinitiate that they are there for the client as a case manager and do not want to do anything to destroy that relationship. Furthermore, the social worker can explore what the client was hoping to gain from becoming friends on social media and help them connect with others to build more appropriate friendships.

Another example would be a social worker working in child protective services and has grown to like a mother who also braids hair for extra income. One day the social worker's regular hair stylist is unable to keep her appointment, so she reaches out to the client in the hope that she can get her hair braided just this one time for a cheaper cost. When the social worker calls the client to ask about being serviced, the client was a bit hesitant because she did not feel well that day but reluctantly agreed. The social worker did not see any harm in this because she paid the client and assumed it would only be a one-time occurrence. What the social worker did not know was that the client has difficulty advocating for herself and saying no to people who are in positions of power such as doctors, mental health therapists, and now her child welfare worker. Not only does this incident create a dual relationship but it does not empower the client to speak up about their concerns and challenge what is being told to her; instead, it takes away her power when social workers should be encouraging clients to feel empowered.

A male therapist has been working with a female client for almost two years with significant progress. At their initial meeting, the therapist noticed how beautiful the client was from her jet-black natural hair in locs down her back, to the curves of her body, and had a hard time not acting on his initial impulse to ask her out on a date. When it was time for termination, the client thanked the therapist who then confirmed how great the client did in treatment followed by asking the client for a date considering he is no longer her therapist. The client was flattered at the therapist's advance and decided to begin a romantic relationship. The therapist not only overstepped professional boundaries by asking to take the client on a date but continued to violate boundaries by continuing the relationship. The therapist has gotten to know the client in a very intimate way with the client sharing her fears, traumas, insecurities, and being extremely vulnerable in relationships with men. Some would say that since the therapeutic relationship has been terminated that there is no harm done. WRONG! Social workers cannot engage in a dual relationship where there is a risk for potential harm or exploitation of a client.

Sasha has been a therapist for almost 10 years and has been working with Anthony for nearly a year. Anthony is always pleasant during sessions, has been trying to stay later than his session time to keep "talking" to Sarah, and has been asking Sarah questions about her personal life which she has impulsively answered thinking nothing of it. At the beginning of a session, Anthony shows up dressed in business casual attire and a dozen red roses in a vase and presents it to Sasha saying that he appreciates everything that she has done for him during their sessions. Sasha is both shocked and uncomfortable at the gesture, but she accepted the roses and conducted the session. There are some "red flags" that Anthony may be interested in a dual relationship with Sasha and it is Sasha's responsibility to not only look out for the red flags but to also redirect Anthony when they are presented. When Anthony makes attempts to keep talking to Sasha during sessions, Sasha can redirect him by stating at the beginning of sessions the importance of ending on time and by keeping a watchful eye on the time and attempting to end a few minutes early to allow time to wrap things up. When Anthony inquires about Sasha's personal life, it is essential to redirect the conversation, explore the root of the question, and reiterate that the focus of sessions is to help Anthony and not discuss her personal life unless there is some benefit to him. Lastly, when Anthony showed up to the therapy office with roses, Sasha needed to be assertive and firmly state that although the gesture is appreciated, that these kinds of gifts cannot be accepted and request that Anthony take the roses back. If the roses were delivered, Sasha could have left the roses at the front desk and immediately discussed proper protocol with Anthony. This may sound harsh, but Sasha has to be mindful not to give

Anthony the wrong impression about their relationship. If Anthony wanted to express his gratitude, he could always write a letter to either Sasha or the program director. Some agencies have specific rules about accepting gifts, for instance an employee cannot accept anything over a specific amount of money which leaves clients the opportunity to be creative and make gifts with little to no monetary value.

Another common boundary violation is self-disclosure. Self-disclosure is the sharing of information about yourself to someone else either verbally or nonverbally. Self-disclosure can be done intentionally or unintentionally. For example, if a married therapist is having a session with a client who notices the therapist wearing a wedding band, this is unintentional self-disclosure. If the client points this out to the therapist, it could be a way to generally build rapport as the client may also be married but in no way should the therapist disclose intimate details about their marriage as if they are meeting with a friend. On the other hand, verbal self-disclosure can be a therapist who is meeting with a client who is sharing relationship issues and the therapist discloses how they were in a toxic relationship along with specifics about the impact it had on them. There are times when self-disclosure is appropriate but only when it benefits the client.

While in a therapy session, a social worker is meeting with a client who mentions difficulty finding a contractor to remodel their bathroom. The social worker has a friend who is an excellent contractor and does not see any harm in sharing the word in an effort to help their client. Although this seems harmless as the social worker is trying to connect the client with a decent contractor to help with their remodeling dilemma as it is becoming increasingly stressful for the client, there is a conflict of interest to steer your client to a friend as the client working with the contractor could impact your relationship with them.

Not all dual relationships are unethical and some are unavoidable. For instance, if the social worker attends the same church as a client but did not realize until well into their relationship, this could be considered a dual relationship. Depending on the size of the church and ministry affiliations with each other, this dual relationship may only be brief such as passing one another after Sunday morning service, which does not pose an ethical violation.

As previously mentioned, accepting gifts from clients can be damaging but it is important to mention that not accepting a gift can also be damaging to the therapeutic relationship depending on the culture. For instance, some cultures find it customary to give gifts as a sign of appreciation from one to another. Although social workers may be cautious in accepting gifts, it is important to learn about your client's culture so that you are maintaining firm, healthy boundaries with your clients but at the same time you are not offending your clients which can have a negative impact on your ability to work with them. This is where cultural awareness comes into social work practice, as a social worker you must continue to learn about different cultures formally and informally.

It is good to know the possible consequences with social workers violating the code of ethics. These consequences could be someone contacting the state board or the National Association of Social Workers (NASW) and reporting a code of ethics violation. In the event this happens and depending on the ethical violation, the social worker could have their license suspended, could lose their license, their job, or even their private practice.

*I always wondered
why somebody doesn't
do something about
that. Then I realized
I was somebody.*

- Lily Tomlin

Social Work
In Movies

There are numerous movies, shows, and documentaries that highlight social justice issues and social workers, most of which do not paint social workers in a positive light. These recordings often portray the social worker as lazy, careless, and uninterested in their job or the mission of improving the quality of life of others. Although these are just movies, it can create a perception to society that is difficult to alter. Like any other profession, there are workers who are only interested in collecting a paycheck, but those workers outshine the employees who stay late to complete paperwork, miss their own family events, or wake up in the middle of the night when on call to help with the improvement of the lives of others.

Unfortunately, society does not always have the opportunity to see these social workers.

The movie *Precious* was released in 2009 and is based on the book *Push* by Sapphire. *Precious* tells the story of an overweight, illiterate, New York City 16 year old African American female who is pregnant with her second child while beginning her journey at an alternate school. It is later revealed that Precious has been raped on an ongoing basis by her biological father who fathered her two children. Precious lives with her mother who is extremely physically and verbally abusive which appears to be related to Precious being raped by her father. Precious' mother blames her for getting pregnant and stealing her man. Precious has to meet with the social worker at the welfare office for benefits. This social worker is diligent in confronting Precious' mother about the physical and emotional abuse as well as the ongoing incest that resulted in her two pregnancies. In this movie, Precious' teacher at the alternative school and the social worker appear to have been the needed intervention for not only Precious and her children but also for her mother to begin realizing the impact of her behaviors toward Precious. It appears that no one has looked beyond the surface of Precious' life to explore what may be going on but with the help of the social worker and the teacher, Precious is able to acknowledge the pain and suffering she has experienced throughout her life and to develop a sense of self-worth and purpose.

Miss Virginia premiered in 2019 on Netflix and is based on the true story of Virginia Walden Ford who is an African American single mother in Washington, D.C. who launched a movement to change the educational system due to fear of losing her son to the streets. Neighborhood drug dealers were enticing teenage boys with material items like sneakers, and Virginia became fearful that her son would go down the wrong path due to these negative male influences. Virginia was determined to help her son by enrolling him in a private school in the hopes of preventing him from dropping out of school but was unable to afford the tuition. Virginia learned of a program that has taxpayer academic scholarships and fights to see this implemented in Washington, D.C. Virginia uses her life experience to create a platform to challenge the educational system for educational equality. *Miss Virginia* is an example of how social workers fight for legislative advocacy and equity for the advancement of all people. Social workers lobby to state officials so they can better serve the American people.

The movie *Radio* is based on a true story and follows a young man with a mental disability named James Robert Kennedy. Kennedy, affectionately known as Radio, is unable to read and write and is integrated into the community by the local high school football coach where he finds a sense of purpose when interacting with his high school peers. When his mother suddenly passes away of a heart attack, the school district pushes to have Radio placed in an alternative group placement as he is seen as a distraction to the high school football coach by the community. The school board was more focused on getting Radio out of the school environment than they were on helping and teaching him to ease the adjustment. A social worker would have been a viable resource for Radio throughout his entire life to connect his mother with resources and programs that would be able to teach Radio life skills and integrate into society prior to later adolescence and adulthood.

Lilo and Stitch is a popular children's movie that was released in 2002 and focuses on a lonely Hawaiian girl named Lilo who adopts a small dog named Stitch. Lilo encounters a social worker named Cobra Bubbles after her parents died in a car accident. Bubbles is a former CIA agent with a larger stature and muscular body tone who later becomes a social worker. During Lilo and Bubbles first encounter, Bubbles comes into the house looking around the home and questioning Lilo's older sister Nani about leaving Lilo alone. Bubbles also tells Nani that he is the person that is called when things go "wrong." Before leaving the home, Bubbles tells Nani that she has three days to change his mind about his first impression. This encounter was brief, but it depicts what so many believe social workers to be, merely people who invade your personal space and make demands. In this instance, a social worker should not judge the family they are working with but should instead focus on rapport building with the family to see what their needs are. When a social worker takes the time to get to know the client and their family, they are developing a trusting relationship which makes it easier for the family to share their needs, concerns, or even their fears about what could happen. In this movie, Lilo is lonely and is in need of a friend. The social worker could have taken the time to get to know the family and offer resources to help Lilo develop friendships and ease Nani's burdens related to caregiving.

The 1974 film *Claudine* follows a single African American woman named Claudine who lives in New York City with her six children while secretly working in the suburbs and receiving public welfare benefits. During this time, the public welfare system did not allow women who were receiving assistance to work. Claudine was outwardly expressive that the assistance she received from welfare was not enough, so she had to work to support her children. In the film, Claudine's children see the social worker coming up the street to the apartment building and warn Claudine of her arrival. It is at that time that Claudine and her children begin to scuffle around the apartment and switch out their better appliances, like the iron and toaster oven, along with hiding their nicer rug that sits under the coffee table. It becomes second nature for the children who are noticeably aware that they are not allowed to have nicer things and that the social worker will be checking for these things and asking questions about Claudine working or having other potential deductions.

The social worker was a white middle aged woman who called herself Claudine's "friend" but was seen looking around the home and prying into her personal life asking about whether Claudine is seeing a man and more specifically about his contribution to the household. By Claudine's response it would be no surprise that she felt disrespected and violated by the social worker asking her if she is sleeping with a man and if he is bringing her things. This is an example of the historic public welfare system that was seen more as punitive instead of helpful. In Claudine's experience, the public welfare system will view her as lazy if she stays home receiving public welfare and is seen as cheating the system if she works outside the home. Where is the middle ground for this struggling mother? This movie is yet another example of the social worker aligning more with the system and not the needs of the family. Of course, the social worker has a job to do and is held to the standards of the organization she is employed by, but it is her responsibility to work collaboratively with

Claudine to identify her goals, to help her achieve these goals, and offer resources to improve her and her children's quality of life.

In the 2009 film *The Blindside*, a young boy named Michael has lived in multiple foster homes from which he runs away. A woman notices Michael's misfortune and lack of adequate clothing and offers to take him into her family home which eventually leads to seeking guardianship after Michael's father passed away. It was at that time the woman learned that Michael was taken away from his mother who has experienced substance abuse at the age of seven and that her whereabouts are unknown. The woman also discovered that Michael tests in the 98th percentile in protective instincts leading him to become an offensive lineman on the high school football team. Although the woman's motives were questioned as a means to recruit him to college football teams, it was evident that Michael needed someone consistent to care for and to love him. With the instability in his family of origin and instability with foster homes, Michael seemed to be a case that was not thoroughly followed by the child welfare system as no one searched for him when he ran away from the foster home. Michael may have been labeled a "runaway" due to his history of leaving foster homes, making him less likely to be tracked and cared for. Children like Michael can fall through the cracks once they are placed in foster homes because they are "placed," but there is so much more that can be done from a social work perspective. Michael could have benefited from a social worker who was able to not only secure a placement from him but one who advocated for him to receive adequate mental health treatment due to years of abuse and neglect.

The Trial of Gabriel Fernandez follows the Los Angeles, California child welfare case of Gabriel Fernandez with several reports of neglect and abuse which lead to his death in 2013 at only eight years old. Gabriel lived with his uncle and his uncle's partner for some time and then moved with his grandparents prior to moving in with his mother and her live-in boyfriend in 2012. Gabriel's family had concerns about his mother taking him because of a history of neglect towards her children. During Gabriel's eight months living with his mother and her live-in boyfriend, he was severely abused and tortured. Gabriel started a new school where he caught the attention of his teacher after asking if it were normal to be hit with a belt and with further exploration, Gabriel stated that he would be hit with the buckle of the belt on his bottom resulting in bleeding. As a mandated reporter, Gabriel's teacher called the child abuse hotline where she inquired about whether Gabriel's statements were reportable and it was confirmed that a report needed to be made. Gabriel's case was assigned to a new social worker who, with other child welfare agencies, did not find an adequate justification to remove Gabriel from the home.

As the months went on, Gabriel's abuse worsened as evidenced by patches of hair missing from his scalp and a busted lip from being punched in the mouth by his mother. On May 22, 2013, Gabriel's mother called 911 stating that Gabriel was not breathing. When the ambulance arrived, Gabriel was transported to the hospital where it was determined that Gabriel sustained a series of injuries which included a cracked skull, broken ribs, and had BB gun pellets lodged in his skin. At the hospital, it was announced that Gabriel was brain dead and he passed away just two days later. During the trial, it was discovered that Gabriel was forced to eat cat litter and was locked in a cabinet in his mother's room as punishment. This case sparked media attention due to the severe nature of the ongoing abuse. Although social services were involved in Gabriel's case, it appears that the system failed to protect him from the person who was supposed to love him most, his mother.

Unfortunately, cases like Gabriel's are what society knows about social workers, hence leaving social workers with a bad reputation. The four social workers who worked on Gabriel's case were fired and later criminally charged with child abuse and falsifying records. The records also indicated that the safety programs were working and did not detail the abuse. Not only is it the responsibility of the assigned social worker(s) to document everything that is pertinent to the well-being of the children, but to stand as an advocate to protect children. Admittingly, it may add another layer of work to the social worker's caseload but there is a responsibility to protect children and to be vigilant of anything that could jeopardize the child's well-being. The social worker's supervisors in this case were also charged as it is the supervisor's responsibility to ensure that their employees are fulfilling their obligation to ensure children's safety. If, for some reason, the supervisor has not done their due diligence, they can be fired and/or legally prosecuted.

The movie *Losing Isaiah* is about an African American woman named Khaila who is addicted to crack cocaine and in the midst of her addiction placed her newborn baby in the trash can in an alley while searching for drugs. The baby was found by a garbage man resulting in the newborn baby, later named Isaiah, being taken to the hospital where it is discovered that he is addicted to crack cocaine and is unable to breathe independently. Isaiah caught the attention of Margaret, a social worker who quickly became fond of him and decided to bring him to her home to join her family which included her husband and teenage daughter.

A few years later, Khaila completed substance abuse rehabilitation treatment and learned that Isaiah was not dead like she originally thought and began to fight to have her son returned to her on the premise that she did not receive notification of Isaiah's adoption. Margaret became upset at the possibility of Isaiah being returned to his biological mother as she had grown to love him and viewed him as her son. Margaret could not understand how there was even a possibility of placing Isaiah in his biological mother's care after he was abandoned, but Khaila presented well in court. The court case grew increasingly intense as racial issues were mentioned and a shortcoming was revealed as Isaiah had not had experiences with African American people.

At the end of the case the judge decided to overturn the adoption and granted Isaiah to return to Khaila. As weeks passed, Isaiah continued to struggle with Khaila as his primary caregiver and mother, resulting in Isaiah not only becoming withdrawn but also having public outbursts. In an effort to do what was in Isaiah's best interest, Khaila asked for Margaret's assistance in raising Isaiah. This movie has several themes for social work including the significance of including culture in child welfare, specifically when placing children in homes with a different race, and about the power of rehabilitation. Although Margaret may have been considered a middle class two parent household, there were fundamental things missing from Isaiah's upbringing with her and her family. Social workers are trained to assess possible cultural differences to teach foster parents how to embrace these differences while connecting them with resources to do so in an effort to have the best possible outcome for the child.

The Netflix original movie *Hillbilly Elegy* is the memoir of J.D. Vance who sheds light on the social problems of his family and his hometown Middletown, Ohio. After serving in the military and while attending Yale Law, Vance received a call from his older sister stating that his mother was in the hospital following a heroin overdose. Although Vance was concerned about his mother's well-being, he was reluctant to return to his hometown due to his strained relationship with his mother and his upcoming law internship interviews. Vance drove for 10 hours to be with his family, but when he returned he realized that his mother was being released from the hospital and did not have anywhere to go. Vance used his resources and managed to get his mother into a substance abuse treatment program after charging the first two weeks on several of his credit cards. After witnessing this, Vance's mother left stating she was not a charity case.

In the midst of Vance's frustration, his sister told him that she was working on forgiving their mother and that things did not start with them. Vance learned that his mother and maternal aunt witnessed domestic violence at the hands of her parents and even saw her mother set her father on fire following a heated argument. Vance began to see his mother in a different light and began attempting to help her. Vance was also forced to reflect on his childhood, which included verbal, emotional, and physical abuse at the hands of his mother to the point that she threatened to crash a speeding car while both her and Vance were in it. Vance's grandmother decided to take him to live with her during his teenage years and would often yell at him. During a car ride, Vance's grandmother had a tough conversation with him about the importance of getting an education and the need for him to make it in life but he had to want to succeed. That was a turning point in Vance's life where he began excelling at school and working in local stores.

Vance later became a lawyer and is now a contributor on CNN. His memoir focuses on the Appalachian values of his upbringing. At several points in the movie, a social worker's intervention would have been appropriate. A social worker could have been a much needed resource when Vance's mother lost her job as a nurse due to substance use. The social worker could have provided needed resources to the family, including connecting Vance's mother with substance use treatment and ensuring Vance was temporarily in a safe home, such as his grandmother's while his mother received the much-needed treatment. A social worker could have continuously monitored the family and taught Vance's mother the skills to maintain sobriety, including developing a relapse prevention plan. Social workers should be the first line of defense and be proactive with services and resources instead of being reactive when things go astray. Vance's life story demonstrates the influences of family dynamics and values, the impact of addiction, and the long-term effects of childhood turmoil.

There may be times
when we are powerless
to prevent injustice, but
there must never be a
time when we fail to
protest.

- Elie Wiesel

Advocacy in Documentaries

In recent years, several documentaries have been created to reveal global problems from maternal health disparities to human trafficking, the school to prison pipeline, to the loopholes of the 13th Amendment and the role of social workers in the judiciary system. *The Naked Truth: Death by Delivery* investigates the maternal health disparities and how African American women are up to four times more likely to either die during childbirth or shortly thereafter than their white counterparts and up to 12 times more likely in New York City. *The Naked Truth: Death by Delivery* explores why African American women are dying at extremely higher rates than white women although the United States spends more on healthcare than any other country in the world. The root cause of African American maternal mortality is underlying racism, which is a systemic issue. The documentary features a variety of birth workers from doctors, nurses, midwives to doulas, and even families of women who have experiences with the maternal health disparities.

One woman shared her story about her daughter who went to the hospital after her water broke at five months pregnant with twins. Her daughter had previous children and was noted to have a weak uterus. The mother was heartbroken and confused as she had assumed the hospital would effectively treat her daughter and granddaughters, but that did not happen. The daughter was encouraged to have a vaginal delivery in which she hemorrhaged, leaving her and her twin daughters dead. This documentary is eye opening and sheds light into a major systemic issue of black women dying due to professionals not listening to their needs including their pain, concerns, or even taking the time to explain the rationale for medical interventions opposed to just doing what they feel is appropriate. Social workers can act as advocates and even be professional doulas or midwives to educate women and their families about birth, create a birth plan, and advocate in the delivery room.

The United States Department of Justice defines human trafficking as "a crime that involves exploiting a person for labor, services, or commercial sex. The Trafficking Victims Protection Act of 2000 and its subsequent reauthorizations define human trafficking as: "a) Sex trafficking in which a commercial sex act is induced by force, fraud, or coercion, or in which the person induced to perform such act has not attained 18 years of age; or b) The recruitment, harboring, transportation, provision, or obtaining of a person for labor or services through the use of force, fraud, or coercion for the purpose of subjective to involuntary servitude, peonage, debt bondage, or slavery." Human trafficking occurs throughout the United States and is estimated at 20-40 million people nationwide. In 2019, the United States National Human Trafficking Hotline identified 22,326 victims and survivors of human trafficking with over 14,500 people in sex trafficking alone.

Risk factors for human trafficking include: poverty, mental health, substance use, gang involvement, online vulnerability, runaways and homeless youth, people with disabilities, children in the child welfare or juvenile justice system, and people in the LGBTQ community. Social workers who work in the field of human trafficking can work in several capacities beginning in preventative services. Preventative services include educating the community about human trafficking including the factors that can contribute to human trafficking, potential warning signs that everyone can look out for, and the long-term effects of human trafficking including psychological and physical trauma and providing outreach to people who are currently involved in human trafficking. Beyond preventative services, social workers work with survivors of human trafficking by advocating for intervention and treatment programs, connecting survivors with adequate housing, food assistance, and medical care along with psychiatric treatment. Social workers may also provide therapy to survivors to process their trauma.

Murder to Mercy: The Cyntoia Brown Story shares the story of 16-year-old runaway, Cyntoia Brown, who was forced into prostitution by her abusive boyfriend who was reportedly a drug dealer. Brown entered into a man's car after being solicited for sex and was taken to the man's home. Brown reported being fearful that the man would kill her based on his behaviors, resulting in her shooting the sleeping man in his head. At that time, Brown was considered a prostitute and not a victim of sexual predators, resulting in her conviction of murder and robbery, therefore she was sentenced to life in prison during her 2006 trial. Brown's case was reopened, and it was discovered that she was born with Fetal Alcohol Spectrum Disorder (FASD) as her mother drank alcohol during pregnancy resulting in alcohol related neurodevelopmental disorder and impaired functional ability which is comparable to people with mild Intellectual Disability.

Following media and celebrity attention and with increased pressure, Brown was granted clemency and released after 15 years in prison. Specifically within this case, social workers would be needed to advocate that Brown's FASD and functional ability be taken into consideration during criminal proceedings along with her history of trauma associated with being a runaway adolescent who was forced into prostitution. Social workers working in the judiciary system are responsible for finding alternatives to jail such as rehabilitation programs for lower-level offenders, supervising offenders in the community, and eliminating the cause of criminality within communities. Social workers can be responsible for providing mental health services to inmates and readjustment services to help former inmates with community integration. Social workers can also be victim and child advocates performing trauma screenings, providing crisis counseling, preparing children to testify in court, supporting both children and parents during medical evaluations, and providing psychoeducation to parents.

Unfortunately, oppression and racism is entangled in the United States legal system and as social workers we must embrace the core value of social justice by helping people in need and also by addressing social injustice. The Thirteenth Amendment to the United States Constitution states in Section 1 that "Neither slavery nor involuntary servitude, except as a punishment for crime whereof the party shall have been duly convicted, shall exist within the United States, or any place subject to their jurisdiction." Section 2 states that "Congress shall have power to enforce this article by appropriate legislation." Although slavery was legally abolished in 1865, the movie *13th* sheds light on how the Thirteenth Amendment is nothing more than a formal policy that has a major loophole which is stated as a punishment for crime that the person has been convicted of.

During the Civil Right era, blacks were arrested for minor crimes such as loitering which would become a punishable crime. In the Nixon administration, there was a war on drugs where drug addiction and dependency were viewed as a crime instead of a public health issue. For instance, people of color, particularly black people, were jailed for having low levels of marijuana. It was also during the Nixon administration that black people were viewed as enemies and were strategically associated with marijuana where it was heavily criminalized. During the Reagan administration, cocaine began infiltrating communities. Crack cocaine was an inner city issue but cocaine was seen as a suburban issue. There then became mandatory sentences for powder cocaine which would disproportionately affect people of color, particularly black people, forcing them into servitude. The 1994 Federal Crime Bill was focused on the expansion of prisons, mandatory sentences, and the three strikes and you're out which federally mandates prison for life sentences which again disproportionately affected black people. Social workers can organize community members and advocate to Congress about the racial disparities in the criminal justice system along with instituting reform programs.

How wonderful it is that nobody need wait a single moment before starting to improve the world.

-Anne Frank

Famous
Social Workers

As previously mentioned, Jane Addams is known as the "mother" of social work, but there are other notable social workers. Mary Ellen Richmond, born in 1861 and died in 1928, is another social work pioneer. Mary Ellen Richmond's parents died when she was very young resulting in her being raised by her grandmother, who was a women's suffrage advocate, and her two aunts. She grew up surrounded by social and political beliefs, suffrage, and racial problems. In 1889, she became the assistant treasurer of the Charity Organization Society (COS) Baltimore chapter. The Charity Organization Society was the first organization to develop the social work profession which included providing services to those who were poverty stricken and disadvantaged.

Richmond continued to work with the COS and conducted research studies focused on families and the resources available to widows along with their interactions with the social welfare systems. Richmond wrote the book *Social Diagnosis* in 1917, where she expressed what social casework was and how environmental factors play a key role in the development of one's life. She believed in what is now called the person in environment theory, that in order to work with a person you must first explore the person's environment which includes but is not limited to their family and those closest to them like their churches, schools, and jobs.

Ida B. Wells is another well-known civil rights activist, journalist, and teacher. She was instrumental in launching the National Association of Colored Women, was unofficially a founding member of the National Association for the Advancement of Colored People (NAACP), and organized the first suffrage club for women. Wells was born a year before the Emancipation Proclamation and was active in racial issues throughout the south. After her friend was lynched, Wells launched an investigation into lynching and became the first person to document the lynching of an African American. Wells traveled abroad spreading the word about lynching and openly addressed white women who were involved in the suffrage movement but ignored lynching. Wells also wrote *Southern Horrors: Lynch Law in All Its Phases* that spoke about white men's sexual violence against black women and black men being attacked by white mobs for having consensual sex with white women.

Edith Abbot was known as an educator, author, and social reformer. Abbot was the dean of University of Chicago, School of Social Administration and was the first woman in the history of the United States to become the dean of a graduate school. During the great depression, Abbot worked closely with her sister who was also involved in social problems and public welfare to address social issues like immigration and child labor. In 1927, Abbot became the co-founder of the Social Service Review publication. From 1925-1927, she was the president of the American Association of Schools of Social Work and was even appointed to the Wickersham Commission (National Committee on Law Enforcement and Observance) later in the 1920s. Lastly, she was named the president of the National Conference of Social Welfare.

Frances Lomas Feldman was born in Philadelphia to Jewish immigrants and initially considered a career in medicine before deciding to study social work. Feldman worked as a social worker for years, teaching several courses like policy, administration, and social welfare history and wrote several books including *Human Services in The City of Angels: 1850-2000*. Feldman was so committed to the social work profession that her husband left his job as a research chemist and became a social worker specializing in gerontology. Feldman conducted research in the 1970s about the discrimination cancer patients faced in the workplace that included withdrawal of health insurance coverage, denial of promotions, and demotions which resulted in a change in employment legislation.

Mary Church Terrell was born the daughter of former slaves and her father was one of the south's first African-American millionaires. Terrell is one of the first African-American women to earn a college degree, graduating from Oberlin College in 1884. Terrell's friend was lynched in Memphis, Tennessee in the late 1890s by white people simply because his business was in competition with theirs. This event ignited Terrell's passion for activism and she started her fight for women's suffrage and racial equality. Terrell also worked alongside Ida B. Wells during anti-lynching campaigns. In 1896, Terrell became one of the founders of the National Association of Colored Women (NACW). In an effort to share her firsthand experience with discrimination, Terrell published her autobiography, *A Colored Women in a White World*.

Dr. Dorothy Height is known for being a social worker and civil rights activist. She won an orator contest with her prize being a college scholarship resulting in her applying and being accepted to Barnard College in New York. As the beginning of the school year approached, the college rescinded Height's acceptance due to meeting their quota for black students. Height remained persistent and earned two degrees from New York University. She later enrolled in Columbia University and the New York School of Social Work for her postgraduate education. Height joined the Young Women's Christian Association (YWCA) and the National Council of Negro Women. While serving in leadership roles at the YWCA, she worked directly on issues of racial injustice and gender equality. Height became the first director of the YMCA's new Center for Racial Justice in 1965, which she ran for over 20 years. Dr. Height fought tirelessly for racial justice and actively joined in the Civil Rights Movement. Dr. Height was awarded the Presidential Medal of Freedom by President Bill Clinton in 1994 and was awarded the Congressional Gold Medal by President George W. Bush in 2004.

Edward Franklin Frazier is known as both a sociologist and a social worker. Frazier is a graduate of

Howard University and has taught at several schools from high school to the collegiate level. Frazier attended the New York School of Social Work and then became the Director of Social Work at Atlanta University. Frazier is described as a critic of Jim Crow and has published several literary works about white racism and its effects on black people. Some of Frazier's published work includes *Black Bourgeise*, *The Pathology of Race Prejustice*, and his doctoral dissertation *The Negro Family in Chicago*. Throughout Frazier's career, he stressed the importance of social activism in relation to the social work profession especially during the 1920s when racism was prominent and even legal. Frazier was vocal about the need for social workers to speak out against injustices instead of going along with it.

George Edmund Hayes was the first African American to graduate from New York School of Philanthropy (currently Columbia University School of Social Work). Hayes had an interest in civil problems that directly impacted black migrants from the south which resulted in his doctoral dissertation *The Negro at Work*. While black people were migrating to urban areas, Haynes served as a social activist regarding their living conditions. Haynes also co-founded the Committee on Urban Conditions Among Negros with Ruth Standish Baldwin in 1911 in an effort to improve the working conditions of black people. This committee later became the National Urban League.

Not only was Whitney Moore Young, Jr. a teacher and coach, but he later graduated with a MSW from the University of Minnesota in 1947. Following his MSW he began working at the Urban League in Minnesota where he later became the Executive Director from 1961-1971, taught social work, and in 1954 became the dean of the

Atlanta University School of Social Worker. Young was an advisor to multiple United States Presidents including Richard Nixon, Lyndon Johnson, and John F. Kennedy and was also an organizer of the March on Washington in 1963. Young was a noted civil rights pioneer, social worker, and statesman who served as the first dean of the School of Social Work at Atlanta University, now known as Clark Atlanta University (CAU) at 33 years old. He served as the president of the National Conference on Social Welfare in 1965 and the president of the National Association of Social Work in 1969.

Not all of us can do great things, but we can do small things with great love.

- Mother Teresa

Research

A survey of 102 social workers was completed specifically for this book and gives insight into their role as social workers and the social work profession as a whole. There were no social workers with an Associate degree, 2.94% held a Bachelor's degree, 93.14% held a Master's degree, and 3.92% held a Doctorate degree. Based on this data, a Master's degree is the most popular degree held among social workers. Aside from these social workers having either a master's level or a clinical license, 66.67% of the social workers are licensed and/or have certifications. The certifications vary greatly depending on the social worker's area of specialty. One social worker is also a Certified Revenue Integrity Professional (CRIP). The CRIP guarantees a high standard of expertise in individuals working in the healthcare field with regard to billing and documentation of services rendered.

Several social workers surveyed were certified in therapeutic modalities such as Dialectical Behavioral Therapy (DBT), Cognitive Behavioral Therapy (CBT), Family Therapy, Eye Movement Desensitization and Reprocessing (EMDR), Marriage and Family Therapy, and Gestalt Therapy. Three social workers have advanced degrees, one in education, one in human sexuality, and another with a Juris Doctor. Other social workers had the following certifications: Perinatal Stress Disorders, Nephrology social work, clinical social work supervisor, adoption assessor, clinical anxiety treatment professional, grief therapist, violence against women and children, equine assisted mental health, adult mental health screener, drug and alcohol counselor, Attention Deficient Hyperactivity Disorder (ADHD) Clinical Services Provider, somatic experiencing practitioner, trauma art therapy, Trust-Based Relational Intervention, and Rubenfeld Synergist. One social worker is also a registered play therapist and another is a licensed acupuncturist. A few social workers hold NASW certifications: Board Certified Diplomate in Clinical Social Work (DCSW) and the Academy of Certified Social Workers.

The surveyed social workers hold a variety of positions to include: psychotherapist, behavioral health consultant, clinical coordinator, family advocate, integrated behavioral specialist, volunteer and hotline coordinator, school behavior counselor, outreach coordinator, social work supervisor, lecturer, strengthening families coordinator, associate director, program manager, intake casework supervisor, disability determinations counselor, dean, affiliate chaplain, foster home developer, assistant director, field director, project assistant, bereavement therapist, and the ethics chair for a social work professional organization. In an attempt to gather information and insight from social workers in various stages of their career, the survey notes that 24.75% of social workers have been in the field for less than five years, 26.73% of social workers have been in the field from five to ten years, 17.82% have been in the field for 10-15 years, 7.9% have been in the field for 15-20 years, and 22.77% have been in the field for more than 20 years.

Finances are an important factor when deciding a career and it was valuable to inquire about yearly income when surveying social workers. Twenty percent of social workers make less than $40,000, twenty-six percent make between $40,000-55,000, thirty-two percent make between $55,000-70,000, fourteen percent make between $70,000-85,000, two percent make between $85,000-$1000,000, and six percent make over $100,000. Social workers only licensed in Pennsylvania surpassed other states at 71.57%, those licensed in both Pennsylvania and New Jersey were 2.94%, those in New Jersey, Kentucky and Georgia were at 1.96%, California was at 2.94%, New York at 4.90%, Missouri at 3.92%, and the following states: Delaware, Oregon, Mississippi, Texas, Maine, Massachusetts, Illinois, and Ohio tied at 0.98%.

Over 12 specialty areas were reported with mental health and clinical social work ranking at 75.25%. Administrative social workers at 17.82%, child welfare at 25.74%, community work at 21.78%, consulting at 10.89%, forensic at 6.93%, gerontology at 12.87%, legislative at 0.99%, medical at 28.71%, school at 13.86%, substance use at 24.75%, and the remaining included victim services, homelessness and housing, interdisciplinary legal, intellectual disability, teaching, and research.

When asked about the social worker's career goal, 2.9% of the participants skipped the question, while others had a variety of responses. Career goals included going into private practice, being a traveling social worker, becoming a program director, owning a nonprofit mother/child shelter, becoming a director of compliance, becoming a trauma therapist, becoming a Licensed Clinical Social Worker, working in research and administration, program manager at a community health clinic, hospice, medical social work, supervisory position, non-profit management, opening and operating a holistic trauma healing center, publishing articles, and humanizing systems. Less than five social workers' have the goal of retirement and two social workers reported that they were already at their career goal.

Future social workers can anticipate many things while preparing to fully enter the social work field, but there are many things that cannot be anticipated prompting the next survey question which is ,"What is one thing you wish you knew before becoming a social worker?" Several of the responses were related to the stress, burnout, and exhaustion that can be associated with the profession. To tell future social workers that the social worker life is easy and burnout is not present would be a blatant lie, so knowing the potential for burnout before going into the profession will help future social workers build their career with the internal goal of reducing their risk of burnout and creating a balance. Several social workers reported the difficulty of balancing their personal and professional lives along with the long-term impacts of compassion fatigue.

There were several points that were made related to schooling such as learning that there are programs that will pay for your MSW degree, obtaining more information on macro and clinical social work tracks, tailoring field placements to align with your overall goal, the quality of education can feel low, and that the division of micro and macro work can be misleading as activism and solidarity should be a part of all aspects of social work practice. It was also mentioned that it is okay that you do not know much when you graduate, as much of the learning is done on the job. One social worker noted that they would have liked to know that in order to make money in the field, you have to get more degrees and licenses, while another mentioned that they wished they knew about the importance of supervision and consultation along with how to supervise others.

Multiple social workers reported feedback related to the financial aspect of social work like the low pay, average salary in general, knowing how to negotiate salary, and knowing your worth and advocating for yourself. Others reported wishing they knew the importance of joining professional organizations, the expenses associated with maintaining your license, how to build a strong social work network, and all the opportunities that exist within the field. One social worker mentioned they wish they knew more about insurance prior to becoming a social worker, which can come in handy when linking clients to resources and coordinating discharge planning. Some wished they learned more about traveling or international social work, had a clearer vision or goal of what they wanted to do in social work, knew how to develop a business plan, and knew the challenges, such as marketing, associated with having a successful private practice. One social worker wished they knew that sometimes the regulations within the system that a social worker has to work under can make the job more difficult as most of these regulations were not written by social workers and or people who have training in social work. A few social workers found that they wished they knew how much they would love it, how rewarding this work could be, and how they would be blessed by serving others. Two social workers pointed out how little people outside of the social work field understand and appreciate the field.

Several social workers mentioned the harsh reality of social work for some, which includes that there is no real shared vision of ending socioeconomic oppression and how social work is a white system where black social workers have less say so and voice to really lead black people. Others would have wanted to learn more about whiteness, law enforcement, and structural racism and how it impacts the work social workers do. The truth is that social work in America was developed using a Eurocentric model, so it has oftentimes fails to take culture into account before diagnosing. As social workers, it is vital before being quick to pass judgement that you view the case from a more comprehensive lens.

Genogram Vignette

Olivia is 25 year old who has been married for four years and has had one miscarriage at five months two years prior. She is currently four months pregnant and experiencing increased anxiety related to fear of losing another child. Olivia has a history of asthma and has not been hospitalized in over five years, has a slightly above average BMI, and has recently had elevated blood pressure causing her to be on the verge of being considered a high-risk pregnancy.

Olivia is working full-time as a registered nurse during the Covid-19 pandemic, which is increasingly stressful due to staff shortages, fear of catching the virus, and fear for her unborn child having complications if she agrees to take the Covid-19 vaccination. Her husband, Bob, is employed full-time as an attorney at one of the city's top law firms. Olivia has a twin brother, a 23-year-old sister, and a 21-year-old brother, none of whom have medical issues. Her 52-year-old father John and her 50-year-old mother Tracey divorced when Olivia was 15-years-old. John has high blood pressure and Tracey has borderline diabetes.

Olivia's maternal grandmother has a history of Stage 2 breast cancer in remission and her maternal grandfather died of lung cancer just two years ago at 75-years-old. Her mother is the second oldest of four siblings (two sisters and two brothers), none of whom has medical issues.

Bob's parents are married. His mother is 51 and his father is 52 with no significant medical conditions. Bob has a 22-year-old sister and a 24-year-old brother whom he has a close relationship with. Oliva's husband is supportive and concerned for her well-being, but struggles to fully comprehend what she is going through causing a strain on their marriage.

Using the information above, create a genogram for Olivia.

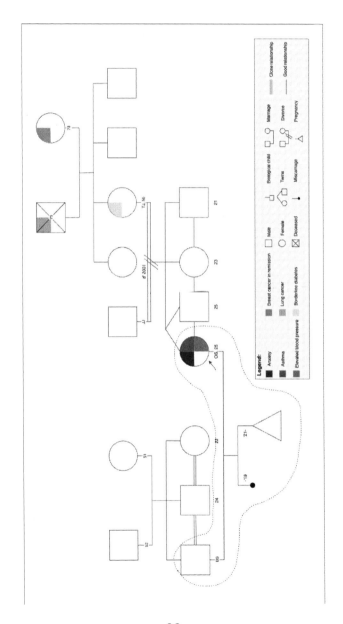

Glossary

- ACE Study: Adverse Childhood Experiences Study found links between childhood trauma and long-term health, behavior, and social consequences among adults.

- Advocate: someone who engages in actions on behalf of someone else as a supporter.

- Assessment: Defined in social work as a means to determine if assistance is needed.

- Autonomy: the ability to self-govern.

- Biopsychosocial assessment: an evaluation of someone's biological, psychological, and social aspects of one's life that could be contributing to one's problems.

- Broker: A person involved in making referrals to connect an individual or a family to needed resources. This requires knowledge and location of resources.

- Case Management: A collaborative process to plan, implement, and coordinate services.

- Civil Rights: According to Britannica, it guarantees equal social opportunities and equal protection under the law, regardless of race, religion, or other personal characteristics.

- Clinical Social Work: According to the NASW, "clinical social work is a specialty practice area of social work which focuses on the assessment, diagnosis, treatment, and prevention of mental illness, emotional, and other behavioral disturbances. Individual, group and family therapy are common treatment modalities."

- Cognitive Behavioral Therapy (CBT): a form of psychotherapy that is commonly used to treat anxiety disorders, depression, eating disorders, martial issues, alcohol and drug use problems, and severe mental illness. CBT focuses on recognizing distorted thinking, evaluating them, and changing behavioral patterns.

- Competent: adequacy, skill, and knowledge in a particular area.

- Confidentiality: information shared between one party and another is to be kept within that relationship. Social workers are responsible to maintain confidentiality except in the event that the client is a danger to themselves or someone else.

- Conflict of Interest: A situation where the social worker benefits from

- Cultural Competence: since becoming competent in another culture, let's define cultural awareness as the one being mindful of not only their differences but their similarities between people. Cultural awareness related to the knowledge of issues related to privilege, oppression, and its potential impact on groups of people.

- Diagnosis: the identification of an illness or problem by thoroughly examining symptoms.

- Diagnostic and Statistical Manual of Mental Disorders (DSM): This book is used to provide guidance in the diagnosis of mental health disorders.

- Dialectical Behavioral Therapy (DBT): an evidenced based Cognitive Behavioral Therapy used to help with emotional regulation, improve relationships with others, and positively cope with stress.

- Discharge Planning: This is used to help transition a client from one level of care to another level of care. Discharge planning begins upon admission and should not be a surprise to the client.

- Duty to Warn: the responsibility of a social worker to alert the authorities or a third party if there is a threat.

- Engagement: the time in which clients are actively participating in treatment.

- Empathy: a social worker's ability to feel what others are feeling.

- Empowerment: the ability to assist clients in realizing their own strengths and their capacity to achieve their goals.

- Genogram: a graphic representation of a family tree including

- Gerontology/Geriatrics: the study of the process of aging and the physical, mental, social, cultural, society, and biological aspects of aging.

- Health Insurance Portability and Accountability Act (HIPPA) of 1996: set national standards for the protection of individually identifiable health information by three types of covered entities: health plans, health care clearinghouses, and health care providers who conduct the standard health care transactions electronically.

- Institutional Racism (also known as systematic racism): refers to racism that is embedded in institutions and systems of power.

- Intervention: the involvement in one's life using a technique or strategy to support, reduce harm, and turn on protective factors. Interventions can be educational programs, parenting classes, connection to resources, creation of policies, psychotherapy techniques, etc.

- Motivational Interviewing (MI): a technique that encourages the client to actively participate in the change process eliciting their inherent motives.

- Mental Status Examination (MSE): an assessment of a person's cognitive and behavioral functioning using the examiner's observations and testing.

- National Association of Black Social Workers (NABSW): Founded in 1968, the NABSW holds to the commitment to provide a safe space for people of color of African descent to confront the issues of racism and oppression.

- National Association of Social Workers (NASW): Founded in 1955, it is the largest membership professional organization for social workers in the world with more than 120,000 members.

- Parent Child Interaction Therapy (PCIT): an evidenced based intervention designed for young children with behavioral problems.

- Psychoeducation: the process of providing education and information to others regarding mental health diagnosis and treatment.

- Self-determination: the ability for clients to make their own decision.
- Social Work Code of Ethics - a document that summaries ethical principles that mirror the social work core values.

Resources

- American Cancer Society 1-800-227-2345
- Battered Women and their Children 1-800-603-HELP
- Childhelp National Child Abuse Hotline 1-800-4ACHILD
- Compulsive Gambling Hotline 1-410-332-0402
- Crisis Text Line: Text SUPPORT to 741-741
- Dating Abuse & Domestic Violence loveisrespect: 1-866-331-9474
- Deaf Hotline 1-800-799-4TTY
- Eating Disorders Awareness and Prevention 1-800-931-2237
- Family Violence Prevention Center 1-800-313-1310
- Grace Help Line 24 Hour Christian Service 1-800-982-8032
- GriefShare 1-800-395-5755
- Hearing Impaired Crisis 1-800-448-1833
- Homelessness 1-800-231-6946
- National Alliance on Mental Illness: 1-800-950-6264
- National Association of Anorexia Nervosa and Associated Disorders 1-847-831-3438
- National Domestic Violence Hotline 800-799-SAFE (7233)

- National Eating Disorder Association: 1-800-931-2237

- National Office of Post Abortion Trauma 1-800-593-2273

- National Runaway Safeline 1-800-RUNAWAY (786-2929)

- National Sexual Assault Hotline 1-800-656-HOPE (4673)

- National Suicide Prevention Lifeline 800-273-8255

- Post Abortion Counseling 1-800-228-0332

- Rape, Abuse and Incest National Network: 1-800-656-4673   S.A.F.E.

- Social Security Administration 1-800-772-1213

- Stop it Now! 1-888-PREVENT

- Suicide Hotline 1-800-SUICIDE (784-2433)

- The Trevor Project: 866-488-7386 (24/7)

- Trevor Project Lifeline 1- 866-488-7386

- United States Elder Abuse Hotline 1-866-363-4276

- United States Missing Children Hotline 1-800-235-3535

- Veterans Association: 1-800-273-8255

- Want to know Jesus? 1-800-NEED-HIM

- Youth Crisis Hotline 1-800-448-46

Symoné Miller is a Licensed Clinical Social Worker (LCSW) who specializes in psychotherapy with adults and the geriatric population. She completed her Bachelor of Social Work at Bloomsburg University of Pennsylvania with a concentration in Children, Family, and Youth. She then received her Masters of Social Service at Bryn Mawr College Graduate School of Social Work and Social Research with the following focuses: Adult Development and Aging along with Children and Adolescents.

Symone' obtained a postgraduate certificate in Cognitive Behavioral Therapy in 2014. She is a member of the Pennsylvania Society for Clinical Social Work (PSCSW). She is also the owner and founder of Expanding Your Horizons, LLC that specializes in therapy and clinical supervision.

Symone' was born and raised in the City of Brotherly Love and Sisterly Affection, Philadelphia, where she resides with her husband.

Divine Legacy
PUBLISHING, LLC.

Creative Control With Self-Publishing

Divine Legacy Publishing provides authors with the guid-ance necessary to take creative control of their work through self-publishing. We provide:

Writing Coaching

Professional Editing

Author Branding

Self-Publishing Coaching

Graphic Design

Website Design

Let Divine Legacy Publishing help you master the business of self-publishing.

Made in the USA
Middletown, DE
14 April 2021

36739423R00066